⊕ An Observer's

Using Pastels

Joan Scott

FREDERICK WARNE

Published by Frederick Warne (Publishers) Ltd, London, 1981

© Frederick Warne (Publishers) Ltd, 1981

ISBN 0 7232 2466 8

Typeset by CCC, printed and bound in Great Britain by
William Clowes (Beccles) Limited, Beccles and London
1499.1180

Contents

Introduction to pastels

There is nothing quite so mouth-watering to an artist as a newly opened box of soft pastels. The lovely colours, some bright, some subdued and subtle, are lying in rows waiting to be picked up and used. A distinction must be made at this early point in the book between what are called soft pastels and oil pastels. The two kinds are completely unlike each other and need quite different treatment in handling. Here it is the use of soft pastels that is discussed.

This beautiful medium has been in use at least since the seventeenth century, but was most popular during the late eighteenth and nineteenth centuries. Some of the artists who have used it brilliantly are Rosalba Carriera the Venetian portraitist, Chardin, Maurice Quentin de Latour and later on, Odilon Redon, whose pastels are quite exquisite and imaginative (see front cover). Degas, of course, had his own superb ways of using the medium, some of which were peculiar to himself. Others using it at about the same time in the late nineteenth and early twentieth century were Vuillard and Manet, and it has become increasingly popular during the last decade.

Permanence of pastel

There is some hesitation by the public in buying pastel paintings because of the erroneous opinion that the medium is fragile. This is quite wrong as, once framed and behind glass, pastel is the most permanent of all. Being composed of pure pigment and a little binder there is nothing to deteriorate or fade, as can be seen in the pictures by the artists already named.

Why choose pastel?

Those reading this book will already have been attracted by the appearance of pastel paintings. They all have a freshness and purity of colour, but one painting can be light, airy and insubstantial, while another can use the complete tonal range and look as rich in colour and tone as an oil painting. The surface appearance will always have an attractive textural finish and a softness and shimmer, as well as a certain amount of transparency, as one colour blends through another.

Uses of pastel—possibilities and limitations

Pastel can be used for sketching either in tone, that is in black, white and grey, or in colour. The sketches can be taken home in order to use them as information from which to paint a finished picture. Pastel is a quick sketching medium, which is a great advantage in an uncertain climate, and for winter landscapes it is ideal as fingers don't have time to get as cold as they do with water-colour. In fine weather conditions it is easier to produce a finished pastel on the spot or before the 'motif' as Cézanne called it. Sometimes this is a good thing as all the subtle colour changes can be noted as well as the exact way in which things grow, but sometimes it can be distracting to have so many changes of light and masses of detail from which to select. It rather depends on the subject of the painting.

One of the delights of using this medium is that it seems like an extension of one's fingers and, as such, it is the most direct form of painting other than finger painting itself. It is a quick and uncluttered medium and requires no tools except one small, hard brush sometimes used for erasing. One good reason for using pastel rather than another medium, particularly for sketching, is its simplicity.

All subject matter can be interpreted with pastel, including the non-representational, but it would appear to have some limitation in the field of miniatures, although this assumption may be proved wrong.

One of the attractions of the medium can also be a disadvantage. This is the ease of handling the pretty colours, ready to be picked up, and the speedy effects to be obtained. Without care, the results can be superficial, slight, and cheap-looking. The dividing line between inspired economy of use and careless superficiality is sometimes difficult for the beginner to see. A pastel done well, with carefully chosen colour and good tonal range, can be superb, but one with ill-chosen, gaudy colour can be both slick and unattractive. Beware of the bright colours in the pre-packed boxes. Don't let their beauty beguile you into using them in the wrong context.

Some of the basics of painting

Before beginning to paint in any medium, it is essential to know something of the basic principles of picture making. There is a theory that art cannot be taught and that anyone wishing to paint should just get on with it. Far from feeling uninhibited, most adults are completely deterred by this approach and feel very confused and discouraged. Obviously, very gifted and instinctive artists will need the minimum of instruction, and information about materials, but for most people, and particularly those wishing to paint in their spare time, rather more help and 'leading on' is wanted. Knowledge of the relevant tools and equipment needed for each medium is the primary necessity and the next is how to use them. Those used for pastel will be discussed in a later chapter.

Composition

Some of the fundamentals to be considered in picture making are composition, tonal qualities, colour relationships and linear rhythm. It is difficult to say which quality is the most important because without attention paid to all of them a picture can fail to make a statement. Although this book is mainly for those who are painting for pleasure, and who will probably wish to interpret landscape, portraiture, still-life and flowers as the subjects appear before them, it is a good thing to realize early on that all concepts of art are abstract qualities whatever may be the subject matter. In other words, before a picture can be thought of as, for example, a barn with trees, decisions have to be made. How much space is this main shape going to take up in the picture? That is, how large is it in relation to the paper or canvas? If it is too big the observer will be overwhelmed, unable to get into the picture at all. If it is too small the shape will be insignificant and the picture will be about space instead. Problem one decided, there is another. Shall this shape be in the middle of the picture or to one side or another? To an experienced artist these problems are quickly sorted out, but to a beginner they can create a real barrier to starting.

The old masters had a formula for composing their pictures, also their sculpture and buildings. This is called the Golden Mean, defined by Euclid as 'a line which is divided in such a way, that the smaller part is to the larger

7

as the larger is to the whole.' In simpler terms this works out to a ratio of about 8:13 and in practice this means that a pleasing balance is achieved by placing the subject of the picture a little to the right or left of centre.

Tonal values

The next thing to think about is tonal balance. That is, the relationship of light to dark. With too little tonal contrast a picture can be insipid and uninteresting. With a large range of tonal contrast it can be dramatic and arresting but a quiet picture requires a smaller tonal range. Nature's vast number of tones can be intimidating and impossible to copy so a compromise has to be made and a range of about seven is workable. Figure 1 shows in charcoal the possibilities of a tonal range.

Figure 1 Table of seven tones; interpreted in landscape

Preliminary sketches

Considering how much thought must be given to the composition and tonal design of the picture, it is wise to make several small sketches first, about 8 × 10 cm (3 × 4 in) in order to sort things out before the actual painting is begun.

Figure 2a The barn is too large within the picture area

Figure 2b This is better but the barn is now a little too small

Figure 2c The barn is about the right size

Figure 2 shows three sketches of a barn with trees. Figure 2a shows the barn as too large; in Figure 2b the barn is too small; and in Figure 2c the barn is about right, the angle is more interesting, and the trees tuck in tidily behind it and at the side.

Colour

The theory of colour is a vast subject and too large for a book of this size. If you can, borrow a copy of *The Art of Colour* by Johannes Itten, published by Reinhold. It is a comprehensive study of colour and, although written in the 1920s, it is still relevant today and makes a fascinating subject for study.

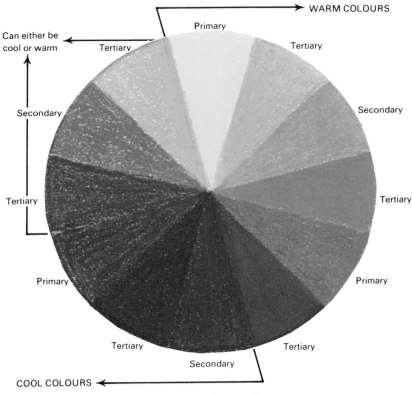

Figure 3 Colour circle

Colour circle

In Figure 3 the usual colour circle that is referred to most often is shown. There is another devised by Ostwald with fourteen divisions instead of twelve. The primary colours, when using pigment and not light, as in theatre spot lighting, are yellow, red and blue. The secondary colours are obtained by mixing yellow and red, making orange, red and blue, making violet and yellow and blue, making green.

By mixing a primary with its following secondary this will give a tertiary, as shown on the colour circle. By adding white to any of these colours, tints will be obtained and by adding black, shades will be obtained. This information is very basic as the study of colour can be a full time occupation, but even so it shows that a great many colours, tints and shades can be made from these simple mixes.

In pastel, of course, the mixing is already done, which makes it harder in one way to obtain a good result because a definite decision has to be made at the beginning as regards colour and tone. Let no one think that pastel is an easy medium because it is quicker than most. Only a limited amount of correction can be made which means that a lot of thought must go into it before a colour is put down.

How to use the colour circle

To return to the colour circle, the warm colours are the yellows, oranges, reds and red violets. The cool colours are the blues, violets and blue violets. Green is neutral but it can be a warm colour with a lot of yellow in it or a cool colour with a lot of blue in it.

Each colour has its complementary, which is the one opposite to it on the colour circle. Two complementaries mixed together will produce grey. This is useful to remember in other media when mixing greens for landscape. If the green is too harsh add a little red which will grey it down and make it more acceptable.

Any three colours adjacent to each other on the colour circle when used in a picture, either on their own or in mixes, will create a harmony, but

Figure 4a Olive Green, tints 0, 4 and 8   **Figure 4b** Terre Verte, tints 1, 5 and 8

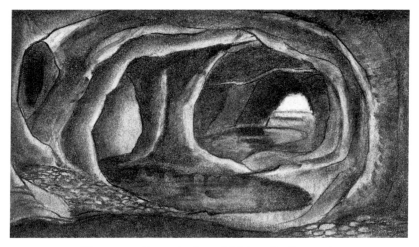

Figure 5 A linear rhythm which is easily discerned

complementaries will create contrast. A discord is where a light colour, such as yellow, and a dark colour, such as violet, interchange their tonal quality and yellow becomes dark by adding black, and violet becomes light by adding white. A little discord in a picture, as in music, can be useful.

Colour is a very personal thing and what attracts one person will appal another. First practices are best carried out in one colour only, using three tones of that colour, that is, a light, medium and dark. When using pastel the colour of the paper can play a part and give one more.

Figure 6 A linear rhythm, but less obvious than that in Figure 5

In Figure 4a, one warm colour, Olive Green, has been used in three tints, 0, 4, and 8 on a neutral grey paper, using various pressures.

In Figure 4b, one cool colour, Terre Verte, has been used in three tints, 1, 5 and 8, on the same grey paper which is common to both and can be seen at the bottom.

Note that the grey paper which is not covered by pastel appears to look cool against the warm colour and warm against the cool colour. This is an example of how a colour will appear to change depending on the adjacent one.

Linear rhythm knits the picture together and gathers it into a whole. From the focal point, or 'point of interest', the eye should be led around the picture and back again by the 'lost and found' linear quality. Sometimes this is obvious as in Figure 5, and sometimes more subtle as in Figure 6.

Materials and equipment

Purchasing pastels

As already mentioned, this book is about soft pastels, as distinct from oil pastels, which are a comparatively new product. Soft pastels are made of pure pigment, finely ground and mixed with the minimum of gum or resin to bind them together, and have a wide chromatic and tonal range.

One firm in England, and Grumbacher in America, make good pastels. The French, German and Dutch are also good but not always easily obtainable. One or two new cheaper makes are now on the market. Try them for softness but they may not be so permanent in colour as the more expensive ones. The English pastels are graded from 0–8, the lightest being 0, and the darkest 8. With foreign makes there is no standardized system, but this information is usually given in the relevant catalogues and leaflets. Some of the colours crumble more easily than others but if the crumbled pieces are kept separately in a small box, they can be used to rub in a ground on a white paper for use as bases for future paintings. This will be explained later.

Pastels can either be purchased in boxes of different sizes or bought separately. The boxes are made up in selections of landscape, flowers, or portraiture but often contain bright colours that are seldom used. It is wiser, if beginning in a small way, not to buy boxes, but to choose a personal selection from the casket kept by all good art shops. Each drawer of the casket is given to a different colour.

Although pastels are expensive, the rest of the equipment is minimal and does not cost as much as that used in other media and so the overall cost probably evens out. All one needs is a board, bull-dog clips, paper, an old stiff brush and fixative, and not always that. A sketching easel is useful out-of-doors, but can be dispensed with at the beginning.

Three tones at least (more later) of each colour chosen, plus a black and a white, should be bought. Although colours can be blended and one put over another, lights and darks cannot be obtained without the right tone. If twelve colours are purchased to begin with and a light, medium and dark tone of each of these colours, this will give a basic palette of 38 pastels, including the black and white. The colours chosen will be different from

those mainly used in oil or water-colour painting because with oil, white will lighten the colour and with water-colour more water is used for lighter tones. For instance, French Ultramarine is a very useful colour, in mixture, for oils and water-colours but is too bright for pastels, generally speaking, except as a flower colour or as a pale tint to be used in the sky.
A useful basic palette could be:

	Tints				Tints		
Yellow Ochre	0	4	6	Hookers Green	3	5	8
Blue Grey	0	4	6	Lizard Green	3	7	8
Terre Verte	1	5	8	Autumn Brown	1	5	8
Indigo	1	4	6	Burnt Sienna	2	6	8
Red Grey	2	4	6	Cool Grey	2	4	6
Purple Grey	2	4	6	Sepia	3	5	8

Black and White

Later additions could include:

	Tints				Tints		
Blue Green	1	5	8	Purple Brown	1	4	6
Yellow Green	1	3	5	Raw Umber	1	3	4
Coeruleum	0	2	8	Warm Grey	3	4	5

(The tints used in this chart are according to the English grading system)

Storing pastels

If you decide to buy the made-up boxes there will be no problem in storing them for inside work. If each pastel is replaced in its original position each time the painting session is finished they will be ready for the next time they are needed.

If not bought in the boxes, every pastellist has his own pet way of storing his pastels, both when they are new and when they have been broken and used, and there is great therapeutic pleasure in devoting an evening to sorting, cleaning, and tidying them.

The following method will help the beginner. Try to acquire several old cigar boxes. Some tobacconists will sell them very cheaply. On a sheet of stiff paper, as wide as the box and twice as long, mark off at 1 cm ($\frac{1}{2}$ in) intervals. When done, divide every other centimetre into half again. Score all these divisions with a sharp knife. The centimetre intervals are for the pastels, the halved intervals are folded together into an inverted 'V', to make the divisions between. Continue thus until the corrugations fit the box, then fasten to the bottom with small touches of glue.

According to the depth of the box, layers can be added, leaving a space between the last layer and the top of the box to take padding of some sort. The modern plastic padding is very effective. To make it easier to take out each layer when they are in place, glue a small piece of cardboard at each end of each layer. Also, all the layers, except the first, should be stuck to a piece of cardboard to give greater rigidity.

The next delight is how to fill the box. Whether to put all the greens together or whether to file the colours from light to dark etc, it all involves delicious decisions. When packed, keep the boxes closed with two stout elastic bands and try to keep them always upright.

Other kinds of pastel

There are on the market, slightly harder pastels, usually cheaper, which can be useful for accenting linear work and details, and there is also a good selection of colours in Carb-Othello pastel pencils which are useful for sketching but need to be sharpened as they are encased in wood, like lead pencils.

Another material akin to pastel is Conté crayon. These come in short, square sticks in four colours only, sanguine (red earth), brown, black and white. With another colour for the paper, this gives five. However, Conté crayons are slightly greasy, so care must be taken if used with pastel as alterations cannot easily be made. Conté comes in grades of 1, 2 and 3. The best to use is 3, because it is softest; 1 is very hard and suitable only for fine drawing on a smooth paper.

Papers

Papers come in all sorts and colours, and they usually have a 'tooth' upon which to catch the pastel pigment. Mostly it is preferable to use a coloured surface but sometimes white is used for a particular effect. Papers include Ingres Tumba, Ingres Canson, Mei Teintes Canson and Fabriano Ingres, which have a greater or lesser tooth, according to choice. Ingres papers mounted on boards, often used for mounting pictures, are very pleasant to work on but expensive. Also there are several sizes of sketch books containing pastel papers of assorted colours.

Also available is a fine-grained sandpaper which has a beautiful surface upon which to work. It is rather expensive but worth buying for special efforts. A good cartridge paper can be used but it has little bite and so a softer effect with less texture will be obtained. Some water-colour papers are useful, especially if they are 'hot-pressed'. The tinted water-colour papers such as De Wint, David Cox and Turner Grey can also be used. Bockingford, though lovely for water-colour, I find too textured for pastel but some people like it and use it for broad effects and textured surfaces. Some brown wrapping papers are attractive on the non-shiny side but the colour may fade with time. Another paper is a cheap Strathmore which has fibreglass incorporated and this gives a curious textural finish to the painting. Canvas and hardboard can also be pressed into service. Experiment with different surfaces.

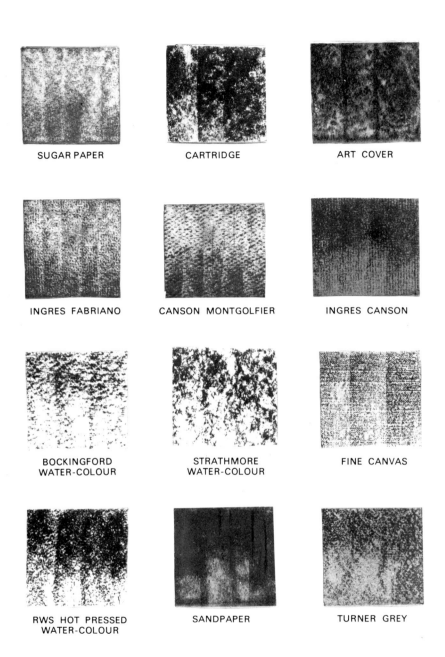

Figure 7 Pastel pulled across different surfaces of paper

Obviously then, the surface of the paper plays an important part. Figure 7 shows the result of the pastel pulled across different papers with different pressures. It is interesting to use a ground laid either by water-colour or crumbled pastel rather than a coloured commercial paper. Figure 8a shows a hot-pressed R.W.S. water-colour paper with a wash of violet and orange. I find the two together give a sympathetic base for many landscape subjects. Figure 8b shows the ground wash of the same violet and orange coming through the pastel in parts, giving a warmth and a depth to the overall colour.

Preparing paper

It has been suggested already that the crumbled pastels be kept, in separate colours if possible. To lay a ground for working on, crush the colours chosen for the ground, scatter them across the paper and rub well in with a damp cloth. When dry, brush off any residue and use as a base for a pastel painting.

The influence of the colour of the paper is considerable if the pastel is used largely in a linear way, or areas of the paper are left for tone, but less so if most of the paper is covered with pastel. Even with these pastel 'paintings' rather than 'drawings' a certain amount of the ground colour is bound to come through because of the nature of the medium, so there is always some influence, either greater or smaller, upon the finished work. Using the colour of the paper as a half-tone can be useful when portraying flowers, as in Figure 9 of daffodils on a greenish grey paper. Notice that the paper *appears* to have a violet tint because it is the complementary to yellow.

The colour of the paper to be used can only be decided by the artist. A pale orange or warm buff is good for summer subjects. It engenders a warm feeling at the outset and contrasts well with blue-greens showing some of the underlying warmth. A pale grey paper may look good for a flower subject of brilliant colours—toning and harmonizing them. A dark brown paper lends itself to autumn landscapes or yellow flowers like buttercups, the yellow looking more brilliant on a dark base. Blue papers are good for winter scenes but there are no rules, it is always a personal choice, and the colour of the paper can either harmonize with the colours of the painting or contrast with it. The harmonies will be quiet and peaceful and the contrast will be vibrant and strong. Figures 10 and 11 show this difference.

Using fixative

Fixative comes either in aerosol cans or a bottle to be used with a mouth spray. It serves to make the particles of pigment coalesce so that they cannot move or fall off the paper.

Whether or not to use fixative is always a discussion point among pastellists. The choice is between the painting remaining fresh and sparkling

Figure 8a Water-colour wash of orange and violet on RWS hot pressed water-colour paper

Figure 8b Pastel produced on the same ground as 8a. The violet helps as a complementary with the corn; the orange gives warmth

Figure 9 The colour of the paper can stand for the half-tone

Figure 10 The colours of the pastels harmonize with the colour of the paper, which can be seen on the extreme right bottom corner, giving a tranquil effect

Figure 11 The effect of colour on a contrasting paper, giving vibrancy

with a chance of some of the pastel falling, or fixing the pigment and losing a lot of the sparkling colour and direct charm. Perhaps it is best to fix at intervals during the course of painting but to leave the top layer and finishing touches unfixed. When fixative is used from an aerosol it should be tried out first to see if the spray is fine and even enough. Sometimes it comes out in large blobs which could ruin the painting.

However, it is a good idea to fix sketches before carrying them home to use as information for future pictures. If a finished picture is being produced on the spot, when finished, place it between two pieces of clean, cheap paper (newsprint if obtainable). Fasten the sandwich to the drawing board firmly with adhesive tape so that it cannot budge and it will travel without fixing. Touch up any bits that may have smudged when safely home.

To fix a pastel, prop it up vertically and gently pass fixative across from top to bottom from about 45 cm (18 in) away. Leave to dry, but never make it too wet in the first place and remember to try out the fixative first.

Equipment for use at home

Equipment for use at home is simple. It is preferable to work with pastels by a window in daylight, but if this is not possible a good fluorescent lamp is a great help, in order to distinguish the colours clearly. A board is necessary, slightly larger than the paper, which can be kept in place by four bull-dog clips. Under the pastel paper should be several sheets of smooth paper of some kind to act as a resilient buffer. A sketching easel is a useful piece of equipment but not absolutely necessary as indoors the board can be propped either vertically or at an angle, whichever is the most comfortable. A cheap trolley is ideal to keep pastel equipment on, as the pastels can be laid out in rows on the top tier and covered with a cloth when not in use. Papers and board can be kept on the bottom tier and the whole can be wheeled to the work table when required. Needless to say, excellent work can be done without this piece of equipment but it does make it easier to have a permanent place in which to keep things.

Equipment for use outside

For outside work, a knee easel is reasonably cheap and works well. It rests on the knees and is anchored under the stool while you are sitting on it and will hold quite a large board. This is much easier to carry about than even a lightweight sketching easel as it folds up into a length of wood about 50 cm (20 in). One essential piece of equipment, though, is a large plastic cloth for catching the pastel which falls to the ground, as it has a habit of doing this in long grass, or on to the carpet. If the painting is done while sitting down, the plastic sheet will protect clothes as well. The permanence of pastel is certainly demonstrated by the fact that once on clothes or carpet it never comes out.

For outdoor sketching and painting a small, folding, lightweight stool is an asset, as it is easier to work sitting down so that the pastels in their boxes can be easily reached when on the ground. A large tote bag is more useful for carrying pastel equipment than the usual sketching bag because the boxes can be kept upright. Into this bag can go the boxes, the knee easel, stool, sketch book, a small jar of ground rice, fixative, plastic cloth, a small wet sponge and towel for cleaning up hands when finished, and a vacuum flask etc, if wanted. The board with pastel papers covered with either newspaper or, preferably, plastic and fastened with clips may have to be carried separately, but even so, the lot can be carried quite easily.

Sketching

As it is unnecessary to carry all the pastels, it is a good idea to have two boxes that are used only for sketching and kept permanently in the bag. Prepare the boxes as for the main supply, but use one box for sky and flower colours only and the other for general landscape. The sky colours can be picked out more quickly when separated from the greens and greys and browns. From the main supply of pastels, break off about a third from each stick, remove from its cover and place in appropriate box. In this way there will be a sample of every colour that has been purchased in the sketching boxes. If a piece is dropped in the grass and lost it is comforting to know that the rest of the stick is safely at home.

A small shallow box or container will hold the pastels as they are used during the sketching session. Some people favour corrugated paper to place them upon but I find a shallow container more practical when in a hurry. A small jar containing ground rice, in which to carry home the used pastels, will clean them before they are sorted and put away at home, clean and bright, ready for the next time they are used.

If there is a window in the house with an uninterrupted view of the sky, keep another 'sky-box' handy on the window sill with sketch book and fixative at the ready. There is nothing so frustrating as having to spend time looking for materials when a good sky is galloping past.

Methods of use

As already mentioned, it is a good thing to remove most of the pastel from the wrapper, keeping only a minimum in the paper, in order to check on the colour and tint when re-purchasing. In this way the pastel can be used broadly, on its side, to establish areas of tone and colour. Later, if and when detail is wanted, the end of the pastel can be used and also the edge. Lines and cross hatching can also be used and Figure 12 shows samples of these various ways of use.

If enthusiasm can be curbed, before beginning to work with the pastels, it will be helpful to make a tint chart, perhaps two charts. One chart should be on white paper, giving the true hue of each colour, but the other, done on a coloured ground of choice, will serve to remind how colour can appear to change according to its neighbour. As the stock of pastels increases, remember to make a tint note on the charts. It helps to realize and remember that what may be the right colour on one paper will appear completely different on another.

Ways of manipulating pastel

There are several ways in which pastel can be used but the common factor to each is the varying pressure used in application.

Rubbing in

One question that is often asked is whether the pastel may be rubbed in. Experienced pastellists can allow themselves a little judicious rubbing in for certain effects but it is advisable for beginners to keep well away from it, as a rather unpleasant, slick effect can be obtained very easily and the sparkle of the colour is lost.

Blending

Working directly gives much more satisfactory results and as one colour is pulled over another the pastels will automatically blend together softly without any rubbing being needed. This is apparent in the method of using the pastel on its side, where one colour can be put over another. Usually it

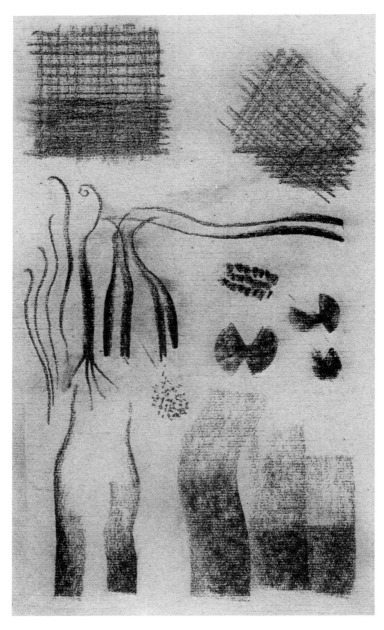

Figure 12 Ways of using the pastel

26

Figure 13a Examples of blending

Figure 13b Examples of strokes laid in side by side

is more effective to work light upon dark but dark upon light can be used, according to circumstances. The colours can also be laid side by side, in patches, but experience is needed to judge the right colours and tones first time with no need of alteration. It is easier to build up from a very lightly applied basic colour pattern, having drawn in the essential composition lines either with pastel or charcoal. This is equivalent to what is called the under painting in oil, but the pastel must be applied with a very light touch in order that the tooth on the paper will not be filled up too soon. Next it is helpful to place the darks, still with a light pressure, and then the lights. Finally the picture is brought together with the lightest and darkest accents. Some of these processes are bound to overlap from time to time, and some pastellists will work in a different order from this, but if the results are successful the technique is of secondary importance. Painting is such a personal thing that no formula can really be given but it helps at the beginning to have a few guiding lines. Figures 28, 29 and 30 will show this method in three stages.

Cross hatching

Another way of using pastel is by using cross hatching or laying short strokes side by side, in which case the edge of the stick is used and one colour is laid next to another giving a vibrancy to the work. In Figure 13 complementary colours are used. Figure 13a shows the two colours pulled one across the other and in Figure 13b the same two colours lie side by side. One method or the other is used according to the effect desired.

Already mentioned is the method of using pastel as a drawing medium, in which case a linear effect is obtained and a large part of the paper is left uncovered as shown in Figure 14.

Different interpretations in pastel

Different approaches in interpretation will need different coloured papers and surfaces, different pressure and different use of pastel. Figure 15 shows how light can be interpreted by subject matter, eg early morning, with the choice of a warm paper and lightly laid in pastel with a close tonal range.

Figure 16 shows a different interpretation of light. By having strong shadows, a brighter light appears to be obtained. In this picture a wide tonal range is used.

In Figure 17, the interest is in colour. This is a picture of largely contrasting colour, giving vibrancy and punch. It can be attractive to some but repellant to others.

A different approach to colour is shown in Figure 18 where the colour is harmonious. Again, according to temperament, this could be found peaceful by some but uninteresting by others.

One interest can overlap another, but it is better to let one theme dominate. In Figure 19 both shape and colour are interests here but because the colour is kept to large flattish areas, the shapes also play a large part.

Tonal shapes, that is, those in light or dark only and very little colour, can also be interesting. Figure 20 shows the patterns made by leaves in a lily pool in black, white and grey only.

Texture can be obtained by using a very textured paper such as Bockingford. This paper is particularly good for snow scenes as, being white, quite a lot of the paper can be left uncovered, as can be seen in Figure 21. Texture can also be built up with cross hatching and other graphic means as shown in Figure 22.

Building up a sketch book

Realism is what most beginners aim for when starting to paint, and there is everything to be said for this. Imagination and abstraction cannot take over freely until a comprehensive visual memory bank has been built up by continual practice in drawing and painting accurately what is in front of us. A good exercise for accumulating this knowledge is to draw and paint outdoor still-life, ie single trees, a bridge, plants, light falling on water, a piece of old wall. In this way study will be concentrated and despair will not set in at having taken on too much, too soon. By building up knowledge with copious sketch-books (always carry one with you) your visual vocabulary

Figure 14 Pastel used in a linear way; using the paper a great deal

Figure 15 Interpretation of light by painting in a high key on light paper

Figure 16 Light interpreted by contrast of tone

Figure 17 Using mainly two contrasting colours gives vibrancy

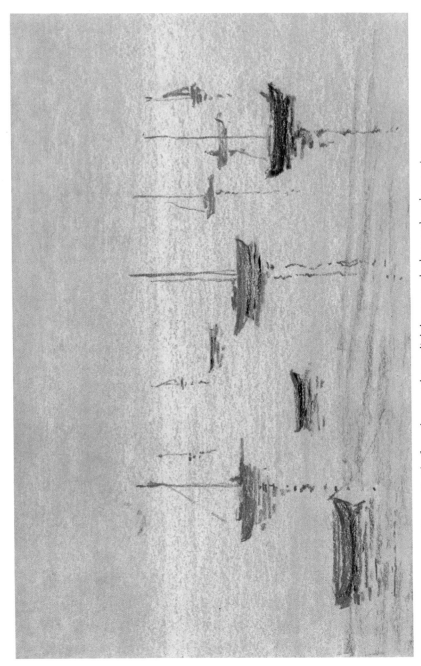

Figure 18 The few colours used, on a slightly warmer background, are harmonious and therefore give a quiet result

Figure 19 How shapes and colours can be combined

Figure 20 Tonal shapes without colour

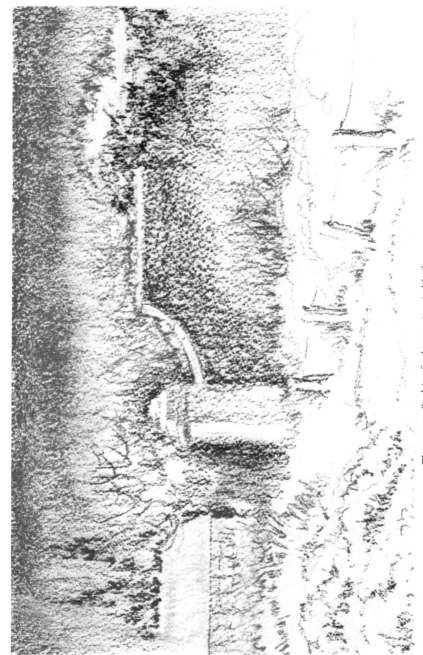

Figure 21 Bockingford paper is suitable for snow scenes

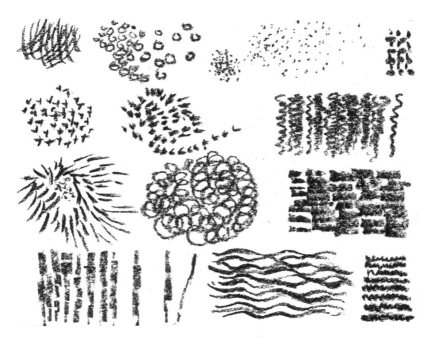

Figure 22 Examples of texture

will be enlarged, and gradually creativity and artistry will creep in when least expected. There are no short cuts, and painting, though enormously pleasurable, is a hard taskmaster and needs constant practice and renewal. When there is no time for painting, practise by drawing something really well, however small.

Never strive to paint like someone else. At the beginning, decide to copy what is in front of you as accurately and sincerely as possible and gradually your personality will emerge and your paintings will be quite different from those of anyone else.

Interest in realism may or may not lead to interest in abstraction or painting from imagination. In any event, the abstract qualities are contained in realism, but are stripped of representational frills in what is called an abstract painting. Many things have to be thought about, such as those mentioned earlier, like tonal balance, line, rhythm, spatial relationships, shape and colour.

Abstraction can be two-dimensional, which means flat shapes without recession as in Figure 23 or it can be three-dimensional which means giving depth within the picture as the painting of a patch of weeds shows in Figure 24.

37

Figure 23 A two-dimensional abstract

Figure 24 Three-dimensional abstract of weeds

Making a start at last

You will be impatient by now to try out the brand new pastels and will feel unwilling to take them out of their wrappers but it must be done in order to use them to their full potential.

Exercises in pressure

Refer back to Figure 12 and try these effects with a dark pastel on a light paper and vice versa. Also try out different pressures on the same paper, and then on paper with different surfaces, to find out which is the most sympathetic for certain effects.

Exercises in monochrome

Following this practice, next try a monochrome, which as the word implies means using only one colour, although if a different coloured paper is used, that will make two. Whereas in oil painting, white can be added to vary the tones of the single colour, and in water-colour, more or less water added to the pigment will alter the tones, with the monochrome pastel there is only the variation of pressure to give the lights and darks. This will go a long way to build up knowledge of how to acquire tone values. For practice, work on a size about 35 × 25 cm (14 × 10 in) and using a dark pastel on a light paper, draw in a simple composition as in Figure 25.

Using a varying pressure, build up the picture, keeping the lightest areas with little or no pastel. Now with more pressure, build up the darks, and then, again with varying pressures put in the half-tones, and lastly, superimpose the darkest darks. Figure 25 has been worked in dark purple on a white paper but try it out in different colours—say yellow ochre on a brown paper, which will mean putting in the lights with the pale pastel and leaving the paper for the darks.

Tonal sketches

Another method which is useful for quick tonal sketches before beginning a bigger picture is to work on a mid-grey paper measuring about

Figure 25 The monochrome completed

Figure 26 A sketch in black and white on grey paper

18 × 12 cm (7 × 5 in) using a black for the darks and a white for the lights as shown in Figure 26.

Corrections

Corrections can be made reasonably easily by lightly flicking off as much pastel as possible with a small stiff-haired brush. Finish the correction by gently applying a kneaded rubber (sometimes called a putty rubber), and then re-pastel. Avoid corrections as much as possible by taking thought first, as the surface of the paper is bound to be disturbed.

Beginning with colour

Mixing and blending

Practice with colour blending will be advantageous in order to discover some of the different effects that can be obtained. Figure 27 shows several variations to practise. In the first row Burnt Sienna tint 3 is pulled over Purple Grey tint 3 and they are roughly the same tonal value. In the second row the colours are reversed, ie the Purple Grey is pulled over the Burnt Sienna. In the third row the same two colours are placed side by side giving a more broken appearance. In the fourth row Burnt Sienna tint o is pulled over Purple Grey tint 6 and in the next row the order is reversed. In the bottom row the two colours are laid side by side.

Pre-selection of the palette

One of the pleasures of painting in pastel lies in the pre-selection for each individual picture. After a while it will be found that some colours are used more than others, as we all have personal preferences, but, as with other media, the fewer colours that are used the more harmonious will be the picture. Do not cut down on the number of colours though, for the sake of it, because, as the colours cannot be mixed in the same way as oil or water-colour, more tints must be used. Pre-selection of the palette to be used in a particular picture saves hunting around for a crucial colour and if these are kept in the shallow container they will be available to be picked up and selected quickly. In selection, if the right colour is not available, compromise by using a similar one, ie cool or warm, but the most important thing is to make sure that the tone is the same. Always try out the pastels on a spare piece of paper similar to that on which the painting is being done.

Landscape

For the first practice landscape, shown in Figure 30, choose a light grey-green paper. The palette will be Blue Grey, tint 4; Terre Verte, tints 1, 5 and 8; Purple Grey, tints 2, 4 and 6; Lizard Green, tints 3, 7 and 8; Yellow Green, tints 3 and 5; Yellow Ochre, tint 6; and Olive Green, tint 8. Figure 28 shows the drawing laid in with the blue-grey pastel and with a light layer

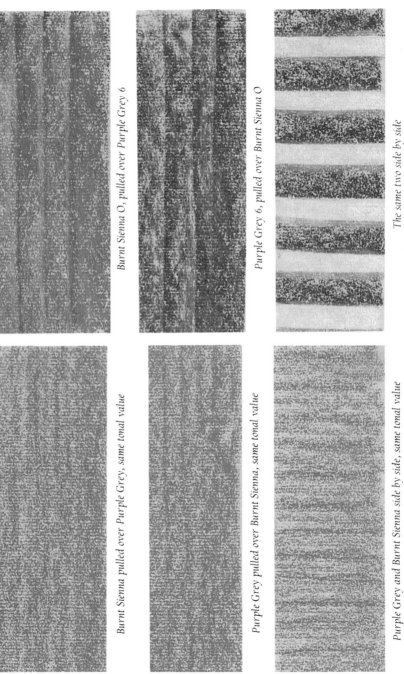

Burnt Sienna O, pulled over Purple Grey 6

Purple Grey 6, pulled over Burnt Sienna O

The same two side by side

Burnt Sienna pulled over Purple Grey, same tonal value

Purple Grey pulled over Burnt Sienna, same tonal value

Purple Grey and Burnt Sienna side by side, same tonal value

Figure 27 Practice in blending

of pastel laid in the relevant areas, using the Blue Grey, Terre Verte 1 and 5, Purple Grey, tints 2 and 4, Yellow Ochre, Lizard Green 3 and 7, Yellow Green 3 and 5. Figure 29 shows the picture developed with some of the darks added and some of the lights and lastly, Figure 30 shows the darkest darks and the lightest lights added and any details to finish off the picture. The thing that brings a picture to life is the last application of lights. Restraint must be used not to put these in too soon. Highlights in still-life and portraits should be held back to the very last. Students often put them in at quite an early stage in order to get an effect but the structural part of the painting must all be done first.

Flowers

Pastel lends itself particularly to flower painting. As one vibrant colour is pulled over another the flower takes on a softness that is not achieved in any other medium, and yet achieves brilliant colour where desired. As with the landscape, begin with a light drawing and lay in of colour. Build up the colours on top of this lay-in, blending and pulling one across the other where necessary. Keep the background to a light or dark neutral grey according to the tone of the flowers. Light flowers will show up better on a dark background and dark flowers on a light. Again, it is a matter of preference but I prefer to see pastel pulled across the background rather than leaving the paper untouched, in the same way that the background in an oil painting of flowers would not be left as untouched canvas. If the flowers are of the daisy type it is a good idea to place the centres first and let the petals radiate from it.

With regard to composition in flower pieces, set flower arrangements do not often make good paintings. They sometimes lack spontaneity and liveliness but if you are an admirer of the Dutch set pieces you will probably not agree. I prefer a few flowers in a simple pot, or flowers with no pot at all, but painted as they grow. If the flowers are a mixed variety keep the larger and more circular ones towards the centre and the more linear and flowing types for the outside of the arrangement. One of the delights of painting flowers is that all the lovely colours that cannot be used in landscapes can be fully exploited here. Figure 31 shows one way of painting flowers. When painting white flowers, brighter backgrounds can be experimented with, as in Figure 32, but never let the background take over from the flowers themselves.

Still-life

Contrary to what most people feel, still-life is one of the most interesting and testing subjects for painting, in any media. What is more, it is always available whatever the weather, which is a great advantage during the dark winter months. The choice is wide open from all the most exciting and interesting things which the world has to offer and the choice can be

Figure 28 First lay-in of practice landscape

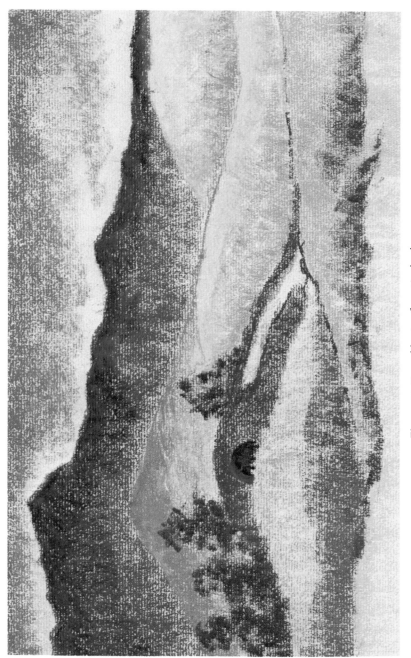

Figure 29 Second lay-in of practice landscape

Figure 30 The finished practice landscape

Figure 31 Flower study

Figure 32 White flowers enhanced by a bright background

personal if painting at home. Natural objects are usually more worthwhile to paint than objets d'art, which are sometimes works of art in their own right and so there seems little point in translating them into paint.

Some of the loveliest things to paint are fruit, vegetables, shells and pebbles. Very often the simplest things are the best, such as the group of green apples in Figure 33. Glass is one of the most rewarding of man-made things to paint and also one of the most difficult for what is left out is more important than what is put in. If the cast shadows and reflections are correctly studied the painting will be an essay in subtle colour relationships and patterns. Try all kinds of lighting—back lighting by day, by placing the group on the window sill. An adjustable desk lamp or spotlight, or even a large torch is useful for giving side-lighting at night which can give a dramatic effect.

Collect pictures of still-life by Old Masters and even new masters, not to copy but to give ideas for subject matter and grouping. Another source of inspiration are the advertisements in the colour supplements. These are often superb photographs of subtly coloured groups of objects. Again, do not copy them but use them as jumping off points for ideas.

Whatever choice is made as to subject matter and grouping, the procedure of pastelling is the same as for landscape and flowers.

Portraiture

Portraiture is a specialist branch of painting in any media and it lends itself well to pastel. It would be a good idea to try your hand at it as your talents may lie in this direction. The only drawback to painting portraits in pastel is that it's easy to get slight, pretty effects particularly when portraying children, but, used well, a pastel portrait can have the same strength as an oil. Eric Kennington's portraits of men in the services during the last war are superb examples. They can be seen in the Imperial War Museum, Kennington, London. Ideally, the picture should be not only a good likeness but a good painting as well and this again is where composition must be given some thought. The portrait can include the arms as far as the hands, perhaps resting in the lap or on the arms of a chair, or it can be just the head and shoulders. If there is a choice, a three-quarters view of the face is good and the portrait must be placed comfortably within the picture plane. As in the composition with the barn the sitter must be portrayed neither too large nor too small within the area of the paper. Oversize can give rather a grotesque appearance. If the sitter is looking to the right, place him or her slightly to the left on the paper and vice versa. As before, one or two thumbnail sketches, in order to get a satisfactory composition, will be useful.

When beginning, lightly mark in the size and position of the portrait and try to keep to this as the work proceeds. Again, if there is a choice, give some thought to the background. A plain background, varying in lights and darks is good, in order to give importance to the sitter but Van Gogh

Figure 33 A simple but effective still-life

combined his sitters with their bright patterned backgrounds superbly, so there are no rules. As so often in painting, it is a matter of personal preference and a lot will depend upon the personality of the sitter. As in still-life, lighting needs to be thought about. A general overhead light such as one usually has to have at evening classes is very daunting. A side light will show up the planes of the face and it will be easier to see the bone structure. A face lit from underneath can make an interesting study. The portraits and family groups of Georges De La Tour, 1593–1652, are worth seeking for this reason. They are available as postcard reproductions. The colours to be used in a pastel portrait will vary with the sitter but there is a good little box on the market, which I find has all the colours necessary for skin tones, put out as a portrait box. This is adequate but a few other colours will be necessary for clothes, hair, etc.

Professional portrait painters like to spend some time with the people they are going to portray, making sketches and getting to know them, but for non-professionals this is not easy and so the summing up of the character of the sitter is necessarily quicker and more superficial.

Having decided on the size, composition and lighting, check the proportions of height to width of the whole head, the line of the eyes, the distance from the base of the nose to the upper lip and from the lower lip to the chin, and the length of the nose. Generally, eyes come half-way between the top of the scalp (not the hair-do) and the bottom of the chin. There may be slight variations from this in different people but children have bigger heads in relation to their features than adults. As none of us is identical, the variations one from another are so slight and subtle that care must be taken to work with more looking and less doing, because too many rectifications will spoil the freshness.

After laying in the lightly laid colour map, it helps to place the eye sockets in a slightly darker pastel than the rest of the face before working the lighter areas of the eyes into this darker shadow, so that at all times the eyes are laid back in their sockets and not just resting on the same plane as the cheeks.

After this lay in the darks, then the lights, and lastly, the darkest darks and the lightest lights and small details. As mentioned previously, the highlights are the very last thing to go in. Place them absolutely correctly as they give the final description of the surface. In particular, the highlight on the nose can alter the shape considerably, according to where it is placed.

Two more things to remember are not to make the whites of the eyes too large or too white as there is a shadow thrown on to the eyeball from the upper lid, and the other thing is to remember that, unless the face is underlit, the top lip will be darker than the bottom one. In Figure 34 you see the portrait laid-in and in Figure 35 it has been brought to a conclusion.

Figure 34 Preliminary lay-in for portrait

Figure 35 Portrait brought to a conclusion

Storing, mounting and preserving

Mounting and framing

The simplest but most expensive way to preserve a pastel painting is to take it to a good framer and let him take over but this can be very costly nowadays. Making frames needs skill and patience and for those wishing to try it, there are specialist articles and books written on the subject and in some areas classes are held in this subject. It is worth thinking about buying frame-making kits which are already cut to size but need to be assembled, but it must be remembered that pastel paintings need glass to protect them which means that beside the frame and the glass, a backing board is also needed as well as a mount to keep the painting away from the glass.

Costs can be kept down by cutting the mounts oneself but even this is tricky so practise first. An essential piece of equipment is a sharp-bladed modelling knife, and a length of triangular metal rod (aluminium angle can be bought at DIY shops) is a great help in giving a support against which to cut. There is on the market, a Dexter Mount Cutter, which some people find easier to manage than cutting a mount with a modelling knife, and this is quite reasonably priced.

Mounting card comes in many colours and several thicknesses. The thinner cards are easier to cut but the thicker ones are better for pastel in order to keep the painting well away from the glass. A good art shop or framer will have samples from which to choose. The colour of a mount to suit a picture is a personal choice but if in doubt choose an ivory, not a dead white and not cream. Cream can be too warm and white can be too cold but ivory will be about right. With a white or pale grey, 35 mm ($1\frac{1}{2}$ in) moulding, incorporating a gold line, this can make a pleasant, standard framing.

To cut a mount, place the card face down on to thick newspaper, glass or thick plastic and mark the inside of the frame measurement, making sure that the corners are square by using a set-square. Cut, using the aluminium angle to cut against, if using a modelling knife. Turn the card over on to its right side and *lightly* mark in with a soft pencil the area of the picture that will be showing. This is 6–12 mm ($\frac{1}{4}$–$\frac{1}{2}$ in) less all round than the actual picture. For a picture 25 × 40 cm (15 × 10 in), a 65 mm ($2\frac{1}{2}$ in) mount all round sets it off but many people think a better balance is obtained by having a slightly bigger measurement at the bottom, say 75 mm (3 in), as it seems to lift the picture up. For a larger picture a larger mount will be necessary and therefore a larger frame. Sometimes a small picture is given more importance by having a very wide mount, but it depends on the picture, as it could be swamped. Having marked the inside measurements of the mount, hold the metal rod on each pencilled line in turn and keeping the knife steady cut against it at a slight angle in order to obtain a bevel. Cut slowly and firmly, being careful at the corners not to let the knife slip beyond the pencilled line. Remove the cut card from the centre of the mount and fasten the picture into the aperture. To do this, place the picture with the right side up, on a flat table. Place the mount over it and when in position, slide the mount and the picture together very carefully to the edge of the table. Fasten a small piece of adhesive tape across one corner of the picture underneath, securing it to the mount. Repeat this manoeuvre for each corner, and when the picture is secure in the mount turn the whole thing over, making sure the surface to receive it is clean, and finally, fasten securely round all the edges with adhesive tape. Put it into the frame, back with hardboard and fasten into the frame either with turnscrews or panel pins and seal with wide gum strip or masking tape.

Some of the thinner papers may need sticking to firm card or board before mounting. If the picture is large and the paper thin it could cockle in time although appearing to be taut at the time of mounting. This is a specialist job and should not be attempted unless one is very skilful, as it can lead to frustration and a spoiled picture. With more painting experience and few failures, the paper can be stuck to the board before the painting begins, or, at greater expense, Ingres boards, which is Ingres paper already mounted on to card, can be bought. This is often used as mounting card as well. Sandpaper will not need sticking to board as it is heavy enough not to cockle.

Storing

Those paintings which are not going to be framed immediately should be kept flat in a drawer if possible, placed between tissue paper or plain newsprint and secured round the edges with adhesive tape so that they cannot shift. So long as the paper on top of each painting cannot move it will not matter how many are laid on top of each other. If no drawer is available they can be kept in a portfolio, but preferably laid flat, as they are inclined to slip when the portfolio is opened.

Pastel with other media

Water-colour

By now, being well launched into using pastel in the orthodox ways, you may find it interesting to try different effects by mixing it with other media. While not advocating that a failed water-colour should be rescued by pastelling over it, it can be exciting to paint a very fluid water-colour and then sharpen it up with pastel on some areas and perhaps drawing the composition together either with pastel line, using Carb-Othello pencils, or a brush line with Indian ink in either Sepia or Black. A brush will have to be used rather than a pen because the nib would soon get clogged with the pastel. This method is best used on a hot-pressed drawing paper like Kent Hollingworth or RWS but if a coarser effect is needed, something like a Bockingford 140 lb can be used. Figure 36 shows this method done on RWS hot-pressed paper.

Acrylic

Acrylic paints, which are water-based and not to be confused with Alkyd paints, which are oil based, can be used to wash over a surface first, on which to build the pastel. Acrylics are waterproof and the first layer will form a very slightly textured surface which, once dry, is permanent and so the cheaper papers like cartridge can be used.

Charcoal

Sometimes, in order to portray a strongly contrasted tonal subject, a good effect can be obtained by building up a tonal charcoal painting on white cartridge paper. Thus a correct tonal monochrome is produced and the colour is provided by pastel afterwards. Make sure to fix the charcoal well before the pastel is added. Figure 37 shows the charcoal monochrome and Figure 38 shows the finished pastel.

Gouache

Gouache is another interesting medium to be tried with pastel. It is an opaque water-based medium and can be done with water-colours by adding Chinese White to each colour, but this means that no rich, strong colours

Figure 36 Pastel with water-colour and brown ink

Figure 37 Charcoal lay-in for the finished pastel in Figure 38

Figure 38 The finished pastel over the charcoal monochrome

can be obtained. It is better to buy about six tubes of Designer's Colours, choosing the permanent tints like the earth colours, the cadmiums and Cobalt and Monastral Blue, a Lamp Black and a Permanent White. Poster colours can be used but they are not so permanent. On the other hand they do not dry up quite so quickly in their pots because they can have a little water poured on top of them when not in use.

Pour a little water into the top of the tubes of Designer's Colours also, before putting them away, and also of acrylics which dry up even faster than gouache if precautions are not taken. The difference between gouache and acrylic in their effect and use, is that gouache will flow more readily, one colour into another, and gives a pleasant matt finish. The layers of colour will move when painted into and can be blended together. Acrylic will flow, if used with lots of water, but not quite so readily as gouache. Of course, once dry, it is completely immovable. Sometimes this is an asset and sometimes it can be a drawback. One colour can be put over another without disturbing the layers beneath.

For those who like to have fun with their painting and to use their imaginations a little, using gouache with pastels has great possibilities but a lot of it is fortuitous and one has to be prepared for a modicum of failures. In this experiment Art Cover paper is used in different colours but white cartridge can also be used, both of which are among the cheaper papers and are easily obtainable from art shops. Choose two gouache colours and select a paper which will either harmonise or contrast. Unless white cartridge is being used, the most important thing is the tube of Permanent White.

The first thing to do is to stretch the paper, as it has to be very wet for the painting. This 'stretching' of the paper will prevent it from cockling which makes painting difficult. Soak the paper in the sink for about ten minutes. Lift it up and drain off the surplus water. Place on the drawing board, which should be 1 cm ($\frac{1}{2}$ in) larger all round than the paper. Mop gently any pools of water but don't rub the paper. Fasten to the board all round with a damp gum strip, half on the paper and half on the board and leave until thoroughly dry. Without wetting the brown gum strip again, thoroughly wet the paper itself so that it is not just damp but really soaking. An old, soft brush will do for this experiment but a large one is best if possible. Keeping your paper wet at all times, mix the colours separately to a thick cream, sometimes mixing the white with them and sometimes using it on its own, and drop the colours into the very wet paper. Don't have too many blobs all the same size all over the paper, but try to compose in a pleasant abstract pattern. Above all let one colour flow into another with complete freedom and no inhibitions. Do not forget to use the white a great deal as this makes the colours flow even more. This is the easy part, all sorts of curious things begin to happen and the paint flows into lovely fern-like shapes. With the use of only two colours and the white, the result should have unified colour. When this process is completed it could look something like Figure 39a, which was done in green and yellow on a blue paper. When quite dry, prop

Figure 39a 'Slosh' with gouache

Figure 39b The other half of the 'slosh' developed

it up somewhere and take a good look. At this point I should like to quote from Leonardo Da Vinci as I find it encouraging. He says, 'I will not refrain from setting among these precepts a new device for consideration, which, although it may appear trivial and almost ludicrous, is nevertheless of great utility in arousing the mind to various inventions.

'And this is that if you look at any walls spotted with various stains or with a mixture of different kinds of stones, if you are about to invent some scene you will be able to see in it a resemblance to various different landscapes adorned with mountains, rivers, rocks, trees, plains, wide valleys and various groups of hills. You will also be able to see divers combats and figures in quick movement, and strange expressions of faces, and outlandish costumes, and an infinite number of things which you can then reduce into separate and well-conceived forms. With such walls and blends of different stones it comes about as it does with the sound of bells, in whose clanging you may discover every name and word that you can imagine.'

So with this 'precept' in mind, keep looking at your 'slosh' and when ready to work on it, remove it from the board and pad well underneath before beginning to work on it. Flower pieces and underwater scenes are usually favourite themes. Pick out salient points with your pastels and don't hesitate to change the colour. One colour of gouache shining through a different coloured layer of pastel can be very attractive.

Any failures need not be wasted as they can be used as under paintings for more orthodox pictures. Figure 39b shows the other half of the 'slosh', carried on further. The lay-in was not identical with 39a obviously but the same colours were used and the two were very similar.

Coloured ink

Coloured inks are lovely things to use but on their own will fade very quickly if exposed to light. If used as a base for pastel they give a glow to the finished work. Cartridge paper can be used for this. Choose two colours only, place a little of each at either end of a glass or plastic palette. Run a roller (those used for lino-cuts are fine) through first one colour and then the other and roll on to the paper. Repeat until the paper is covered. Some of the colour will mix and some won't but the result will be brilliant colour and a slightly textured surface which holds the pastel well. When the pastel is laid on top the inks will shine through in a most attractive way.

By now I hope it has been shown what a fascinating medium pastel can be and what potential it has for life-long interest—happy painting.